Worldwatch Paper 63

Energy Productivity: Key to
Environmental Protection
And Economic Progress

William U. Chandler

January 1985

Worldwatch Institute is an independent, nonprofit research organization created to analyze and to focus attention on global problems. Directed by Lester R. Brown, Worldwatch is funded by private foundations and United Nations organizations. Worldwatch papers are written for a worldwide audience of decision makers, scholars, and the general public.

Energy Productivity: Key to Environmental Protection And Economic Progress

William U. Chandler

Worldwatch Paper 63
January 1985

©Copyright Worldwatch Institute, 1985
Library of Congress Catalog Card Number 84-52719
ISBN 0-916468-63-1

Printed on recycled paper

Table of Contents

Introduction

5

Ancient prophets tried to predict the future with geomancy, a method of divination by drawing dots at random on paper. Energy forecasts, notoriously inaccurate, have been likened to this approach. For all their flaws, however, studies of energy futures continue to command attention. They help define the "state of the world" by exploring where current trends will lead. They influence visions of the energy future, affect research and development expenditures, inhibit or encourage investment in energy supply systems, and thus become battlegrounds for the future itself.[1]

The trends that energy forecasters now draw on paper can affect the entire planet, from Latin American debt to global climate. The higher the predicted demand for energy, the higher the cost of building systems to meet it. The greater the predicted demand for coal, the greater the urgency of averting forest destruction by acid rain and climatic change from carbon dioxide buildup.[2] The wider the error in projected demand, the greater the waste of scarce resources and the worse the failure to provide for other human needs.

The energy events of the seventies caused great upheavals in world energy markets—in effect, a conservation revolution. Like the Green Revolution in agriculture, conservation allowed a brief respite from shortages. It has produced an oil glut, price declines, and time to adjust. But the world of the mid-eighties has relaxed, as it did after the Green Revolution, failing perhaps to make permanent the gains won. A sanguine outlook pervades the energy community as forecasters again draw curves of energy growth bending toward the tops of their graphs. Some suggest a tripling of demand by 2025.[3] If these visions become reality, the world will pay an enormous economic and environmental price.

I thank Marion Guyer, who provided assistance with the research, and Susan Norris, who provided assistance with the preparation of this paper. I also thank Debbie Bleviss, Clark Bullard, Jae Edmonds, Howard Geller, Holly Gwin, and Marc Ross for reviewing earlier drafts of the manuscript.

Supplying new sources of energy takes many years. For this reason, it is crucial that demand scenarios be done, and done well. If more demand materializes than was foreseen, prices will go up and human needs will not be met as well as they could have been. High energy demand scenarios that ignore the potential of conservation, on the other hand, could ultimately cost more than $1 trillion per year in unnecessary energy use. The fiasco in the Northwest United States in the Washington Public Power Supply System exemplifies this danger: more than $5 billion was wasted on unneeded nuclear power plants. Worse, the scenarios could become a self-fulfilling prophecy in which energy consumption has to be promoted to pay for the systems built. The importance of the "consensus" forecasts, then, is that they may come true if leaders around the globe do not implement tough new energy conservation policies.

Affording the Future

Not since the early seventies have analysts so complacently projected a high energy demand future. Alan Manne of Stanford University attributes this, especially the similarity of most official energy demand projections, to "the herd instinct that operates within the community of energy analysts." Nevertheless, a survey of forecasters shows a consensus that worldwide commercial energy demand will increase from about 300 exajoules (EJ) in 1983 to 485 EJ by the year 2000.[4] (Commercial energy excludes firewood and dung, which total approximately 50 exajoules. An exajoule is the equivalent of 163 million barrels of oil, or .95 quadrillion BTU.) The physical magnitude of this scenario numbs the mind. If it comes to pass, the oil output of two new Saudi Arabias will be needed. In addition, the coal production of the world will almost double, and three times as many rivers must be impounded behind hydroelectric dams. Widely cited projections conclude that by the year 2025 the world will need four-and-a-half times the hydro power and three-and-a-half times the coal used today, along with a total of 365 large nuclear power plants. They typically forecast a 125 percent increase in energy demand over the next 40 years.[5]

Among the consequences of using so much energy would be greater
risk of acid rain, carbon dioxide-induced climate change, species ex-
tinction, nuclear weapons proliferation, water degradation, human
dislocation, and capital shortages and debt—connections discussed at
length in Worldwatch Institute's *State of the World 1985*. The consensus forecasts would, within the next century, double the atmospheric concentration of carbon dioxide (compared to pre-industrial
levels) and cause an atmospheric temperature increase large enough
to flood coastal cities and shift rain patterns all over the globe. And
the radical development of hydroelectric power would seriously affect freshwater environments: Fish and mollusk species would be
eradicated, fertile bottomlands destroyed, forests inundated, and
water supplies warmed, depleted of oxygen, and loaded with silt.[6]

The economic prospect of a high energy demand future is similarily
unappealing. Much Third World debt has been incurred to finance
energy imports. Foreign payments for oil consume the largest share
of total export earnings for many countries, including half those of
Japan and Brazil. (See Table 1.) Expensive hydroelectric and nuclear
energy systems have added to this reservoir of debt. Moreover, meet-
ing world energy demand is expected to consume over 7 percent of all
fixed capital investment for the rest of this decade.[7]

This picture of the future is as alterable as it is unattractive. Energy
demand projections are a function of modelers' expectations about
prices, environmental regulations, and the ability of the world to
respond to energy conservation's potential. They represent these
analysts' conceptions of how the world works, not necessarily of how
it could work. All serious projections are made with models that
expose the assumptions that determine their results. One role of
models, in fact, is to make transparent the energy supply, demand,
and policy consequences that nations face.

Including the conservation potential that has been widely demonstrated in microeconomic and engineering analyses greatly affects
energy demand projections. But most models of worldwide energy
demand are, by necessity, macroeconomic. That is, they concentrate

7

Table 1: Energy Consumption in Selected Countries, 1982

Country	Population	Commercial Energy Consumption[1]	Per Capita Energy Consumption	Energy Imports As Share of Exports[2]
	(millions)	(exajoules)[3]	(gigajoules)[3]	(percent)
Argentina	28.4	1.7	61	11
Brazil	126.8	4.0	32	52
Canada	24.6	9.7	395	11
China	1,008.2	17.9	17	n.a.
East Germany	16.7	3.8	231	n.a.
France	54.4	8.5	156	33
India	717.0	4.9	7	81
Italy	56.3	6.2	110	41
Japan	118.4	15.8	134	48
Mexico	73.1	4.2	58	−76
Poland	36.2	5.0	138	20
Soviet Union	270.0	55.0	204	−77
United Kingdom	55.8	7.7	152	14
United States	231.5	75.1	324	36
West Germany	61.6	11.5	187	23
Total	2,880.0	232.0	80	—
World Total	4,585.0	300.0	65	

[1]Commercial energy consumption figures are Worldwatch estimates from 1981 data, assuming little change. [2]A negative figure indicates the percent of exports earned from energy sales. [3]Giga- and exajoules equal a billion and a billion billion joules, respectively. The units are .95 million and .95 quadrillion (quad) BTU, respectively.

Source: World Bank, *World Development Report 1984* (New York: Oxford University Press, 1984).

on broad trends in population, economic output, energy prices, and the interrelationships among these factors. But detailed studies show that the world has barely cut into the conservation potential. Industry, transportation, and housing remain inefficient. Conservation possibilities are so great that economic growth could resume without large increases in total energy use, as Worldwatch Institute projections show. Simply by slowly adopting existing measures, the world could cut the projected energy demand growth rate almost in half—from 2 to 1.2 percent per year.

The global conservation potential can be illustrated in energy portraits of a small number of nations. Some 15 countries, containing about 65 percent of the world's population, are responsible for about 80 percent of all commercial energy use. (See Table 1.) Among these are developing countries such as Brazil, China, and India—nations that have a legitimate claim to greater total energy use. Industrial countries, on the other hand, can substantially raise industrial output, passenger and freight transportation, and household services without greatly increasing energy demand. A single decision in either the United States—to raise automobile fuel economy to 40 miles per gallon—or the Soviet Union—to produce steel as efficiently as Japan does—would save as much energy as Brazil now consumes. Just using the most efficient lights in the United States would save a third of U.S. coal-fired electric energy.[8] Effecting such savings will require great political skill. But conservation's benefits—savings in capital, foreign exchange, environment, and health—will put nations that realize its potential at an advantage. Conversely, the pressures of shortages of capital, foreign exchange, and environmental amenities are likely to force people everywhere to conserve energy.

Continuing Industrial Efficiency Gains

Industrial processes consume more of the world's commercial energy than either transportation or housing. Only in Western Europe does the category of residential and commercial buildings sometimes edge out industry as the most energy-intensive sector. In some countries, particularly the centrally planned economies of the Soviet Union and Eastern Europe, the share allocated to industry approaches two thirds of all energy consumed.[9] Production of basic materials—especially iron and steel, aluminum, paper, chemicals, and concrete—consumes the most. Eighty percent of U.S. industrial energy, for example, is used in the manufacture of these goods. In contrast, agriculture, which is included under the industrial heading, accounts for only 6 percent of sectoral demand.[10]

Industry has provided the largest efficiency gains of any energy-using sector since World War II. A combination of technological improvements, shifts from less-efficient coal to natural gas and oil, and greater production of less energy-intensive industrial products provided industrial countries with an estimated annual rate of efficiency improvements of over 1 percent even as energy prices declined. This rate tripled in western nations after the energy crisis of 1979. Despite the gains, however, an enormous potential for cutting energy costs remains in existing plants, and builders of new production facilities can choose equipment and processes that are considerably more efficient than those already in use.

Japan provides a model of industrial energy efficiency, having made major gains since the early seventies. The energy intensities of chemical and steel production have dropped by 38 and 16 percent, respectively, since 1973, and energy use per unit of output has fallen in every major industry since 1975. The Japanese spent between $25 million and $125 million per year throughout the seventies on energy efficiency in steel production alone. These investments typically paid for themselves in just two years.[11]

The French industrial sector also ranks among the most energy-efficient, and, like Japan's, made large improvements after 1973. Energy intensity in textiles, building materials, rubber and plastics, and mechanical construction fell by more than 30 percent, an annual rate of improvement of more than 3.5 percent. Energy efficiency in paper and steel production increased at more than 2.5 percent per year over the same period.[12]

In the United States, total industrial energy use fell by 6 percent between 1972 and 1981 while paper, aluminum, steel, and cement production increased by 12.8 percent. Thus, the energy intensity of the production of these basic materials fell by 17 percent. As elsewhere, the largest stimulus was higher energy prices, and the major steps taken to cut energy use were "housekeeping" in nature, that is, operational changes usually not requiring substantial capital investments. Other nations that have cut industrial energy intensity include Italy, where energy use in the manufacturing sector declined by 37 percent per unit of output between 1973 and 1981 (5.8 percent per year). West Germany has cut industrial energy intensity at a rate of 2.9 percent per year since 1950, thus making gains even while energy prices declined.[13] During this time, U.S. industry also made gains despite declining energy prices, though they were smaller than after the energy price increases of the seventies.

11

The iron and steel industry exemplifies the global progress made and the potential remaining. Steel-making is both an energy-intensive and a massive enterprise, with annual production totaling about 700 million metric tons. The process consumes 15 percent of all energy used in Japan and the Soviet Union, and over 9 percent of all energy used in Brazil. Altogether, steel manufacturing absorbs about 6 percent of world commercial energy use.[14]

Eighty-four percent of the world's steel is made in 15 countries, with nearly two thirds manufactured in China, Japan, the Soviet Union, the United States, and West Germany. The least efficient major manufacturers are China and the Soviet Union, with China, in fact, using over twice as much energy per ton of steel produced as the most efficient large producers. (See Table 2.)

Italy and Spain rank highest in energy efficiency in steel manufacturing because they are major recyclers. They produce steel using the electric arc, or "recycling," furnace, which uses virtually 100 percent scrap. Recycling enables producers to save up to two thirds of the energy used to produce steel from ore. These two nations partly owe their high rate of recycling, however, to steel-scrap imports from

Table 2: Energy Use in Steel Manufacturing in Major Producing
Countries, Ranked by Efficiency, 1980

Country[1]	Production[2]	Energy Used Per Ton[3]
	(million metric tons)	(gigajoules)[4]
Italy	25	17.6
Spain	12	18.4
Japan	107	18.8
West Germany	43	21.7
Belgium	13	22.7
Poland	18	23.0
United Kingdom	17	23.4
Brazil	14	23.9
United States	115	23.9
France	23	23.9
Czechoslovakia	15	24.7
Soviet Union	150	31.0
Australia	8	36.1
China	35	38.1
India	10	41.0
Total/World Average	700	26.0
Best Technology		
Virgin Ore		18.8
Recycled Scrap		10.0

[1]These 15 countries account for 84 percent of world steel production. [2]Steel production figures represent averages for years 1978 through 1981. [3]Energy totals are for crude steel production, including ironmaking. [4]A gigajoule equals one billion joules, or .95 million BTU.

Sources: Andrea N. Ketoff, "Italian End-Use Energy Structure," and Hugh Saddler, "Energy Demand and Supply in Australia," presented at Global Workshop in End-Use Energy Strategies; other countries from U.N. Economic Commission for Europe and World Bank.

the United States, West Germany, and elsewhere. The world steel recycling rate, despite an abundance of scrap and the advantages of its use, averages only 25 percent, a rate that could be doubled or perhaps tripled.[15]

Steel-making can be made more energy-efficient both by improving existing facilities and by switching to more efficient furnaces. An assessment of investments available to the U.S. steel industry suggests the lucrative potential of conservation the world over. Upgrading conventional furnaces yields high average rates of return: 25 percent per year for continuous casting, 31 percent for waste-heat recovery, and 43 percent for more efficient electric motors. Switching to the electric arc furnace can yield a 57 percent rate of return. In one study of U.S. industry, Marc Ross of the University of Michigan estimated that investments such as these could cut the energy required per ton of steel by a third by the year 2000.[16]

The Soviets recycle little steel and rely heavily on the inefficient open hearth furnace. This technology was used to make some 87 percent of U.S. steel as recently as 1960. Having been replaced by the basic oxygen and the electric arc furnaces, it now is used for only about 8 percent of output. Although it has also almost disappeared from Western Europe, the open hearth furnace accounts for 55-60 percent of production in Eastern Europe and the Soviet Union, where the electric arc furnace provides less than 13 percent of the steel.[17]

China and India also still rely heavily on the open hearth furnace and take little advantage of heat recovery opportunities. Developing countries overall could save at least 10 percent of the energy they use in existing steel facilities by spending only $2-4 billion in conservation retrofits, according to a World Bank study. This investment would pay for itself in energy savings in just one year.[18]

Though installing new steel-making plants provides an opportunity for improving efficiency, it is an uncertain one. The rate of improvement will depend on the rate of demand for steel—a factor difficult to predict not only because of the uncertainty in the global economy but because the industrial market economies presently have about 50 percent excess capacity. Much of the growth in demand, however, is expected in developing countries, and it would be surprising if they did not build their own production facilities. Such plants would provide steel made with cheaper labor, more efficient capital, and lower energy costs, freeing them from foreign-exchange burdens.

Some analysts have displayed pessimism about achieving the great potential for conservation in the steel industry, however. The United Nations Economic Commission for Europe recently forecast that the world's largest steel-maker, the Soviet Union, would fail to reduce the energy intensity of its production below 26 gigajoules per ton before the end of the century. This would only match the current world average and would still be 44 percent higher than Japan's rate today.[19]

Energy conservation in the steel industry clearly depends on energy price. To the extent that market pricing of energy has conveyed the message that energy is precious and expensive, market-oriented countries have conserved. Theoretically, centrally controlled countries could at a stroke mandate the improvement of energy efficiency to any desired level. Studies of these economies, however, show that economic systems never operate so simply, and that complex quota and allocation systems often defeat the best of intentions.[20] In other countries where energy price signals have been stronger, state-owned corporations have usually performed better, as exemplified by Nippon Steel Corporation and Siderbras of Brazil. Greater competition has also created pressure to save not only energy but labor and materials as well. Privately owned "minimills" using the electric arc furnace constitute a dynamic new force for conservation. Major changes like these are difficult factors to anticipate and thus include in models of future production.[21]

The macroeconomic models in vogue today implicitly assume that conservation will not work well. Most assume that the United States, for example, will not reach the current Japanese level of efficiency in steel for 35 years. They assume that the Soviet Union, China, and

India will not match today's performance by the Japanese until after the year 2050. Yet the modelers also assume that half the world's economic output in the year 2000 will be generated by new facilities. Soviet steel-making capacity, for example, is projected to double. And current plans in Brazil call for 50 percent more steel-making capacity by the year 1990.[22] Since growth implies new industrial equipment, there is no good reason why the facilities cannot be at least as efficient as the Japanese steel industry is today. If the growth fails to materialize, which, in the case of steel, is likely, then energy demand still will not grow so much.

15

Indeed, even the Japanese steel industry could economically be 20 percent more efficient. Only a quarter of its steel is formed in electric arc furnaces. Most industry experts expect the minimill to capture a much larger share of the world steel market. Furthermore, if two major constraints on the minimill—the lack of cost-effective technology for rolling thin metal sheets and the need to remove impurities from scrap—are overcome by new technology, minimills may soon produce any type of steel desired. If this happens, a real revolution may take place in steel production.[23]

The prospect for energy efficiency in steel-making, according to some observers, is dimmed by the current economic climate. Staggering from a recession and bad management, the industry cannot afford to invest in conservation, its managers claim, much less in new capacity. This perspective overlooks several basic facts, however. First, when new capacity is needed, conservation investments save capital. Steel mills built around the electric arc furnace, for example, cost only $350-550 per annual ton of steel capacity, compared with $1,500-1,700 for conventional mills using basic oxygen furnaces. Even if the minimill plant cannot obtain scrap (or does not want to depend on imported scrap) and requires a special iron ore reduction facility, the capital cost per annual ton of production totals only $500-900. Adding labor and energy savings to these capital cost reductions gives an overall cost advantage of the minimill in excess of $100 per ton of steel produced.[24]

To assume the world steel industry will forgo the energy-saving minimill in new steel production is to assume that its captains are less than skillful. In countries as technically sophisticated as Brazil, the expertise and technology for achieving the highest levels of efficiency in steel-making exist locally, as they do for other energy-consuming industries.[25] Furthermore, new capacity can outperform the old and capture its markets. This mechanism is already at work, as evidenced by the success of the minimill. To counter this competition, even the major U.S. steel-makers are investing in energy- and cost-saving measures. The retrofits they are making—in continuous casting and heat recovery—offer the steel industry worldwide at least 30 percent energy savings.

Aluminum production is another energy-intensive process, requiring 1 percent of the world's commercial energy. The main energy requirement is for electricity to smelt aluminum from alumina. The efficiency of this technique varies widely around the world. Energy-poor countries such as France are the most efficient, while those with cheap electricity, especially hydroelectric power, use up to half again as much per unit. (See Table 3.) The world average is in the range of 16,500 kilowatt-hours per metric ton. Many producing nations could profitably apply retrofits to reduce the rate to 13,000 kilowatt-hours per ton, but these investments have been slowed because industrial managers assign low priority to conservation. Recycling, moreover, can cut energy requirements by 90 percent. The world aluminum recycling rate is only 28 percent and could be doubled or tripled, but usually requires higher electric energy costs or mandatory recycling laws to come about.[26] Doubling the rate could save almost 1 exajoule per year.

An entirely new, non-electric process of producing aluminum—by coking bauxite in a blast furnace—has been developed by the Mitsui Alumina Corporation of Japan. Announced in 1981, the process has been patented in Japan, where a commercial-scale plant is under construction now, and patents are pending in nine other industrial countries.[27] This technology could not only cut energy costs, it could

Table 3: Electric Energy Use in Aluminum Smelting in Major Producing Countries, Ranked by Efficiency, 1981

Country	Production	Electric Energy Intensity
	(thousand tons)[1]	(kilowatt-hours per metric ton)
Italy	300	13,300
Netherlands	300	13,300
France	450	13,500
Brazil	300	14,000
West Germany	800	14,500
Japan	700	14,900
United States	4,300	15,400
Australia	400	16,000
Norway	700	18,000
Soviet Union	2,000	18,000
Canada	1,200	20,000
Total/World Average	15,900	16,500
Best Technology		
Virgin Ore		13,000
Recycled Scrap		1,600[2]

[1]Average primary production for years 1980-82. [2]Electric energy-equivalent.

Sources: Worldwatch Institute, derived from *Aluminum Statistical Review for 1983* (Washington, D.C.: The Aluminum Association, 1984); David Wilson, *The Demand for Energy in the Soviet Union;* S. Y. Shen, *Energy and Materials Flows in the Production of Primary Aluminum;* U.N. Economic Commission for Europe; José Goldemberg et al., "Brazil: End-Use Strategy," and Rolf Bauerschmidt, "End-Use Energy Strategy for Federal Republic of Germany," presented at Global Workshop on End-Use Energy Strategies. World average from U.N. Environment Programme, "Energy and Resource Conservation in the Aluminum Industry," *Industry and Environment*, August/September 1983.

completely change the current trend toward moving aluminum production to hydroelectric-rich countries in the developing world.

The world now produces about 16 million tons of aluminum, annually requiring the equivalent of 14 percent of world base-load hydroelectric generating capacity. If demand for aluminum doubles by the year 2000, as analysts from the World Bank and the Organisation for Economic Co-operation and Development (OECD) project, electrical demand for production would increase 50 percent, even if energy intensity is reduced to today's most efficient level of smelting. A rate of improvement of 1.6 percent per year in aluminum production energy efficiency is needed to attain this best-technology level by the end of the century. The OECD and World Bank analysts, however, assume only one third this rate of improvement, which is what the world has averaged since 1955. The change realized will depend strongly on electric energy prices and demand for aluminum. As demand increases, more efficiency improvements will be made. On the other hand, electric energy subsidies will reduce conservation.[28]

Assessing efficiencies in the pulp and paper, chemicals, and cement industries is more complex because they encompass greater diversity in product and process. Many energy-saving opportunities are common among them, however. Two techniques typify large, across-the-board savings opportunities: upgrading electric motors and improving heat recovery, including insulation and steam generation using waste heat.[29]

Electric industrial motors consume over 80 percent of all electric energy used in U.S. industry, and a remarkable 40 percent of all electricity used in Brazil. Howard Geller of the American Council for an Energy Efficient Economy has demonstrated the value of improving the ubiquitous motor. His analysis suggests that investing in more efficient motors and motor speed controls in Brazil could save 10,000 megawatts by the year 2000, or over 17 percent of projected new demand for generating capacity.[30]

"More efficient industrial
motors in Brazil could save
10,000 megawatts by the year 2000."

Motors can be made more efficient in two ways. First, using higher quality steel along with better design reduces energy losses due to heating and magnetization of the core. More efficient motors cost only 25 percent more than the average new motor, an investment that in new applications yields a "profit" of 40-200 percent per year, depending on usage rates and electric costs. Most motors are rebuilt rather than replaced, however, because new, highly efficient motors cost four times more than remanufactured units. Despite this differential, in Brazil the energy savings obtainable by replacing motors in need of rebuilding with new ones would provide a rate of return on the extra investment of 10-50 percent per year. Motors can also be improved by adding variable frequency drives to match the speed of heavy industrial motors with the desired power output. Research sponsored by the Electric Power Research Institute estimates that the use of these devices in the United States could save over 7 percent of all electricity used.[31]

19

Papermaking involves considerable pumping of liquids, for which electric motors are largely used. In the United States, replacing electric motors with more efficient ones would typically provide a 47 percent return on investment. Changing to new pulping and lime regeneration equipment would provide 20-40 percent returns.[32] Some of the equipment used in papermaking in the United States is 50 years old, but remains in service because of rapidly growing demand for paper. This situation is the opposite of that in which the steel industry finds itself, where new capacity cannot be justified due to inadequate demand. If demand growth for paper slows, this inefficient equipment could be retired because the old equipment will be more expensive to operate than the new.

The products of the paper industry are becoming "so commonplace, abundant, and cheap that they are almost invisible to consumers."[33] The industry, however, is far from "invisible" in energy use. In the United States, where one third of the world's paper is made, the industry requires about 10 percent of all industrial energy and ranks just behind chemicals, steel, and oil refining in energy use. About half this energy comes from wood waste generated in the production of wood products.

Paper recycling, fortunately, saves about one third of the energy used to make paper from virgin fibers, counting the wood waste used in American paper mills. The United States, however, recycles only 25 percent of all paper consumed, compared with 50 percent in Japan and the Netherlands. Wood-waste energy requirements for U.S. paper production could be cut by at least 15 percent by recycling as extensively as do the Japanese and Dutch. Since the United States uses over half a percent of the world's commercial and non-commercial energy making pulp and paper, the absolute savings would be substantial.[34]

Chemical processing is the world's fastest-growing industry and it already is the largest industrial energy user in the United States. U.S. chemical output grew 50 percent between 1972 and 1981, but at the same time energy efficiency increased 24 percent. Chemical production in West Germany grew 840 percent between World War II and 1982, while energy use by this sector grew only 300 percent. Energy intensity, moreover, has declined rapidly since 1979. Just as in the paper industry, pumping of liquids and heating with steam are required. According to the U.S. Congress Office of Technology Assessment, typical investments by the chemicals industry in electric pumps, heat recovery devices, and cogeneration offer rates of return of 43, 15, and 18 percent per year, respectively.[35]

The production of plastics and synthetic materials dominates the chemical industry in terms of energy use. Significantly, oil is the raw material for these products. U.S. production of olefins for plastics and synthetic materials requires 3.5 percent of all oil used in the country. Only small amounts of plastic are recycled, although this process recovers virtually all the energy embodied in them. Burning waste plastic, the most common method of energy recovery, returns only half the energy used in its manufacture and creates serious pollution problems. Recycling is unfortunately impeded by the fact that post-consumer plastic scrap is difficult to sort and recover. Some chemical products are more easily recyclable. Antifreeze, a major synthetic product, could be recovered and purified. Tires also can be rather easily recovered, and making them with reclaim-rubber uses only

"The energy efficiency of
the Soviet steel industry may not reach
the current world average before
the end of the century."

about 10 percent as much energy as manufacturing them from virgin synthetic fibers.[36] A major policy measure that all countries could implement is to ensure the recyclability of materials. This might include the banning of certain plastic packaging.

21

Cement, an intermediate product in the manufacture of concrete, is the world's most widely used construction material. Its production requires much heating and grinding, but large energy savings can be obtained by grinding and mixing the silicates, calcium, and aluminates in a new dry process rather than in a slurry. The old wet process requires more than 7.6 gigajoules per ton, and switching to the dry process saves nearly a quarter of that. The United States now produces half its cement with this more efficient process, and as a result average energy consumption per ton is down to 6.5 gigajoules. Although new cement-making capacity throughout much of the world uses the dry technique, the Soviet Union continues to rely primarily on the inefficient wet process; institutional resistance is apparently delaying the adoption of the dry process. Australia has not changed either and as a result averages 7.2 gigajoules per ton of cement produced. The energy requirements of both wet and dry processes can be improved by preheating the kilns with recovered waste heat. West European nations combine the dry process with heat recovery and as a result use 25 percent less energy than the United States.[37]

The importance of a comparatively small number of conservation initiatives in industry is underscored by a simple comparison. The Soviet Union, according to the United Nations Economic Commission for Europe, is expected by the year 2000 to increase coal use for steel-making by more energy than Brazil uses today for everything. Simply making the Soviet iron and steel industry as efficient by the year 2000 as the Japanese are now would reduce this increase by four fifths.[38] Most macroeconomic scenarios implicitly assume the Soviets will do no better in this area than the current world average by the end of the century. But because they also assume that the Soviets will double steel production capacity by then, implicit in their forecasts is the installation of technology 20 percent less efficient than the Japanese now use and 40 percent less efficient than available technology that is economical at current world energy prices. Perhaps because the Soviets enjoy energy abundance and do not use market pricing for energy they have little incentive to conserve. But failing to do so will cost Soviet society dearly in lost opportunities to sell oil and earn foreign exchange. They also supply most of the fuel for their East European allies, and any inefficiency in the Soviet Union drives up the cost of supplying these countries.

Worldwide, improvements may slacken, but probably not as much as assumed by most macroeconomic modelers. They project that industrial efficiency in the Eastern Bloc and developing countries will improve far slower than in the OECD, and that the OECD will improve at only about 0.8 percent per year. To reach economical levels of efficiency by the year 2000, a rate of improvement in industry everywhere of more than 2.3 percent per year is needed: this is the rate required to implement the conservation improvements described above. The modelers, then, may be encouraging the world to invest far more in energy supply than is warranted.

Saving Oil in Transportation

Although the transportation sector uses less energy than industry, it uses oil almost exclusively. Thus automobile fuel economy, mass transit, and efficient freight hauling offer the largest oil savings. Private cars consume about 7 percent of the world's commercial energy, or 17 percent of the oil used each year. The United States, in fact, uses 10 percent of the world's oil output as gasoline for motor cars and light trucks.[39]

The transportation sector uses 20-25 percent of energy delivered to consumers throughout Western Europe, North America (including Mexico), and Brazil. In Eastern Europe and the Soviet Union, however, the figure is only 7-13 percent, chiefly because fewer people own cars. Automobile ownership and use is strongly related to income everywhere, even in countries as different as Australia and Japan. Japanese use of energy for transportation is similar to most other OECD countries, despite the fact that it is small, densely populated, and ideal for mass transportation.[40]

23

Affluence, automobile ownership, and fuel efficiency are important issues in both rich and poor countries, even where renewable energy resources are abundant. This fact is evident in Brazil, a country so dramatically divided by income levels that it has been described as "a Belgium inside an India." Car ownership has increased substantially in the last two decades, growing at 7 percent annually even during the last five years, despite the deep recession and high energy costs. Still, the number of cars per person remains only 15 percent as high as in the United States, leaving considerable room for expansion, and ownership among the relatively rich can be expected to continue growing. Even a moderate increase over the rest of the century would double auto fuel demand by the year 2000, given the current levels of fuel efficiency.[41]

The fundamental importance of auto fuel economy can be seen by contrasting current efficiency levels with the technical and economic potential. Fuel economy around the world averages about 21 miles per gallon (8.8 kilometers per liter), though it varies widely. (See Table 4.) The U.S. automobile fleet, not surprisingly, is the world's least efficient, and the newest American models rate only slightly better than the world average for existing cars.

A simple calculation illustrates the profound importance of raising these ratings. If by the year 2000 American cars were as efficient as Japanese cars (assuming saturation in car ownership), world oil use would be 5 percent less than today. Doubling auto fuel efficiency worldwide would permit twice as many cars without increasing energy consumption, or it would allow savings of about 8 percent of world oil output. Achieving this should cost less than $20 per barrel saved; the alternative, producing gasoline or alcohol fuel, will cost $40-60 per barrel.[42]

Automobile fuel economy can be improved far beyond current Japanese levels. Indeed, several major manufacturers have produced pro-

Table 4: Automobile Fuel Economy, Selected Countries, 1982

Country	Autos	Fleet Average	New Cars
	(millions)	(miles per gallon[1])	
Australia	6.3	19	24
Brazil	9.7	20	24
Canada	10.6	18	27
East Germany	2.4	27	32
France	17.8	27	32
Italy	17.7	24	31
Japan	39.0	31	30
Soviet Union	8.0	26	29
United Kingdom	15.6	22	28
United States	125.4	16	22
West Germany	23.2	22	28
Other	77.0	n.a.	n.a.
Total	353.0	21[2]	25[3]

[1]Actual mileage on the road. Data may not be strictly comparable due to differing national testing procedures. [2]Based on 80 percent of the cars in the world. [3] Based on 70 percent of the new cars in the world.

Sources: International Energy Agency, *World Energy Outlook* (Paris: OECD, 1982); International Road Federation, *World Road Statistics 1978-82* (Washington, D.C.: 1983); United Nations Economic Commission for Europe, *An Energy Efficient Future: Prospects for Europe and North America* (London: Butterworths, 1983); Motor Vehicle Manufacturers Association, *World Motor Vehicle Data Book, 1983* (Detroit, Mich.: 1983). Automobile Club d'Italia, *World Cars, 1984* (Pelham, New York: Herald Books, 1984).

totype cars that obtain up to 93 miles per gallon. Models that get 78 miles to the gallon have been built by General Motors (a two-passenger car) and Volkswagen (a four- to five-passenger model).

The economics and acceptability to consumers of these cars is not yet clear, however. Indeed, General Motors and Ford have sought exemption from the minimal U.S. standards for 1985, though Chrysler opposes any changes in the law.[43]

Improving automobile fuel economy both would extend oil supplies long enough to develop renewable energy sources safely and would make the use of renewable energy feasible. Brazil, for example, chooses to concentrate on alcohol fuels, and if its cars are no more efficient by the year 2000 than they are today, over twice as much fuel will be needed. Supplying this requirement with alcohol would require 16-20 percent of the total land area committed to crop production in 1980. Brazilian physicist José Goldemberg and his colleagues conclude "these are formidable requirements which are probably impossible to achieve in reality."[44] Even today's alcohol fuel output, which meets about 3 percent of Brazilian total energy needs, apparently has caused some social and environmental stresses.[45] If within the next five years, however, Brazil required all new cars to get 31 miles per gallon, projected consumption would grow "only" 43 percent. This level of fuel economy in new cars could reportedly be achieved in short order without major capital investments in Brazil's auto industry, the seventh largest in the world. If Brazil mandated a new-car fuel economy of 47 miles to the gallon, fuel demand would by the year 2000 be slightly lower than today.[46]

Many options can be incorporated to achieve these high fuel economy levels. Reducing auto weight can save 25 percent of the energy used in the typical car. Engineering more efficient engines can yield another 20 percent improvement, as can the installation of efficient continuously variable transmissions (CVT). General Motors and Fiat both will soon begin production of the CVT in France, though they have experienced difficulty with the manufacturing process. Simply installing the most efficient tire available on the market today would improve the fuel economy of most cars by 1-3 miles per gallon.[47]

Rolf Bauerschmidt of the University of Essen has shown how West German fuel consumption could be cut by a fifth by the year 2000 while the auto fleet grows by 12 percent. He assumes that new cars will mainly be diesel-fueled vehicles getting 36 miles per gallon. Gasoline-powered cars would not grow in number but would become more efficient, achieving 29 miles to the gallon. These goals are easily within the realm of technical feasibility, though reaching them may require government intervention. He also assumes that travel by train will double, a more uncertain prospect. Rail passenger-travel remains at about the same level as just after World War II, and the service, though excellent and improving, is heavily subsidized.[48]

Where transportation systems are inadequate or nonexistent, there are even greater opportunities to use mass transit to cut or avoid growth in energy use. Traveling by train is inherently more efficient than using a private car. In West Germany, for example, railroads use only one fourth as much energy as cars to move people an equal distance.[49] The autobus is comparable in efficiency. No mode of passenger transportation, however, is both more flexible and more efficient than the van pool. (See Table 5.)

Technical improvements are also possible in mass transit systems. East European trains, for example, perform more efficiently than West European ones. If Soviet railways achieved a similar technical level of efficiency, savings of 50 percent could be made.[50]

Developing countries face a particularly difficult task in providing transportation services. Strapped with debt and under pressure from the International Monetary Fund to cut domestic expenditures, budgets for providing additional bus services have been reduced, and rail services are frequently out of the question because of their high initial capital cost. But failing to provide mass transportation costs dearly if the lack of service is made up privately with motor cars.

Nigeria illustrates this dilemma. The lack of transport services is evidenced by the use of only a half barrel of oil equivalent per capita in transportation in 1980, less than a sixth the level in West Germany. One Nigerian analyst projects this will rise to 3.2 barrels of oil equivalent per capita by 2010. Wide use of mass transit would greatly

Table 5: Fuel Efficiency By Passenger Transportation Mode, Western Europe

(kilojoules per passenger kilometer)

Van Pool	400
Rail	400
Bus	450
Car Pool	650
Automobile	1,800
Airline	3,800

Sources: Worldwatch Institute estimates and United Nations Economic Commission for Europe.

reduce this projection, but the current service is so poor that it strongly encourages the purchase of automobiles. Potential passengers are deterred by buses filled to crushing levels. Many already commute four hours per day on mass transit and, despite crowded roads, find private transport more convenient when they can afford it. Most cars carry only two passengers, though average capacity is five. Yet roads are so crowded in Lagos that in 1978 legislation was enacted that permitted vehicle use only on alternate days. Predictably, the law was circumvented by those who could afford second cars.[51]

An alternative that reduces congestion, saves energy, and cuts government transportation costs is the jitney. Jitneys are comparatively small vehicles that offer shared rides along major routes. Small fleets of these taxicabs, vans, or trucks are usually operated by private owners. Though problems sometimes arise in regularity of service and in neglect of less profitable routes, these are generally outweighed by large increases in low-cost transportation service. Profit-making private jitneys often operate at full seating capacity, usually during rush periods. Although they have the potential for lowering the efficiency of public transport by skimming the most profitable routes, they can also reduce governments' need to buy large vehicles to meet rush-hour demand. These large vehicles would be used either at less than full load—or not at all—during most of the day. Thus jitneys can save commuters the energy and capital costs inherent in private cars and can save governments some of the high capital and operating costs of mass-transit vehicles. Studies report the successful operation of jitney services in a dozen cities around the world, from Hong Kong to Buenos Aires.[52]

Most countries face trade-offs in the movement of freight, which often burns up more energy than passenger transport. The Soviet Union, in fact, uses 75 percent of all transport fuel moving freight. Freight transport can be reduced by both shifts from truck to rail as well as increased efficiency of transport trucks, which carry half or more of the freight in the United States, Europe, and Brazil.[53] Soviet freight is mostly carried by rail, which is why the country has the highest freight transport efficiency, though the use of coal in locomotives instead of diesel fuel makes them less efficient than would otherwise be expected. Replacing Soviet gasoline-powered trucks with diesel units would also bring improvement.

Freight transport over the road is expected to grow in most major countries, so the importance of increased efficiency of transport trucks is central. U.S. truck transport is inefficient due to poor aerodynamics and poor load factors, which have historically been due to a bad regulatory policy that required many truck operators to return empty to their destinations. Technical improvements such as airfoils, however, can improve efficiency by 6 percent, with turbocharging adding 12 percent and radial tires 10 percent. In Brazil, a doubling of efficiency of trucks is considered feasible. This would permit at least twice as much road freight transport without any increase in fuel consumption.[54]

A basic problem in both the United States and Brazil is the decline of railroads. In Brazil they are poorly managed and inefficient, while using the U.S. rail system is slower than sending freight by highway, due to poorly maintained rail beds and poor freight transfer systems at switchyards. A major shift back to rail would be costly and is

unlikely without the impetus of much higher fuel costs or government intervention. Developing countries, however, will probably
want to give priority to rail transport over highway construction.
Water transport is far more efficient than either rail or truck, if waterways already exist. The construction of waterways to compete with
rail has not always been an effective use of capital, but in Brazil, water
transportation along the Amazon and the coast to the industrialized
south probably presents a better alternative than construction of
either rail or highways.[55]

29

Worldwide, the future of oil use depends most on the future of
transportation, especially the automobile. Because saving oil can help
secure the future of the automobile as well as relieve economic and
environmental pressure, it is only prudent to seek the highest economically achievable rates of fuel efficiency. Governments will play a
major role in the future of transportation because generally they alone
possess the resources to provide alternative transportation and they
can regulate fuel economy. They will also greatly affect freight transportation energy use, albeit less directly. Fuel economy levels of 30
miles per gallon are achievable everywhere by the end of the century;
levels of 50 miles per gallon are attainable shortly thereafter. But the
world will not realize this important potential if governments adopt a
hands-off attitude.

Although market signals for energy prices are vital to increased fuel
economy, the market alone will not bring about economically feasible
levels—for two main reasons. The first is that consumers do not
consider fuel economy as a top priority when buying cars unless fuel
prices are increasing rapidly. Second, when an oil emergency does
occur, automakers cannot quickly supply efficient cars. Typically, five
years are required to re-tool to make new cars more efficient.

Thus, the market alone cannot guarantee future energy efficiency or
even promote completely rational economic behavior in the short
term. It falls to governments to ensure that auto fuel efficiency, the
single most important oil conservation measure in the world, is

achieved. To effect this, a combination of market pricing, fuel taxes, and efficiency regulations will be required.

Improving Buildings and Appliances

Energy use in buildings around the world ranges between extremes. In most industrial countries, oil, gas, and electricity warm or cool air, heat water, provide light, refrigerate food, and run appliances such as ranges, washing machines, and televisions. In developing countries, wood or dung is the principal fuel, used mainly for cooking. More efficient stoves would both reduce wood waste and improve the quality of life in these areas, but their use is somewhat problematic. Measures for halving energy use in industrial nations include improving and replacing appliances, especially furnaces and air conditioners, and reducing heat loss from poorly insulated buildings.

The opportunities for conservation are greatest in North America and Western Europe, where rates of energy use in the buildings sector reflect both the climate and high income levels. These countries have a long way to go before completely adjusting to the energy price increases of the seventies. Nonetheless, improvements since 1973 in the OECD countries in this region have been impressive. (See Figure 1.) Denmark, the most improved of these nations, has reduced energy use in buildings by 32 percent, an impressive record considering that the area of buildings heated increased by 23 percent during the period. Canada and the United States also achieved major reductions—19 and 16 percent, respectively. France, Sweden, and West Germany registered smaller percentage reductions, but they started from a more efficient base.[56]

The Swedes realized most of their savings by investing in weatherization, while 75 percent of the improvements in the other countries resulted from no-cost or low-cost changes such as turning down thermostats. Lee Schipper of the Lawrence Berkeley Laboratory reports that technical efficiency of Swedish houses far exceeds that of the United States, even after adjustment for climate. Swedish homes,

Kilojoules/Degree Day/Square Meter

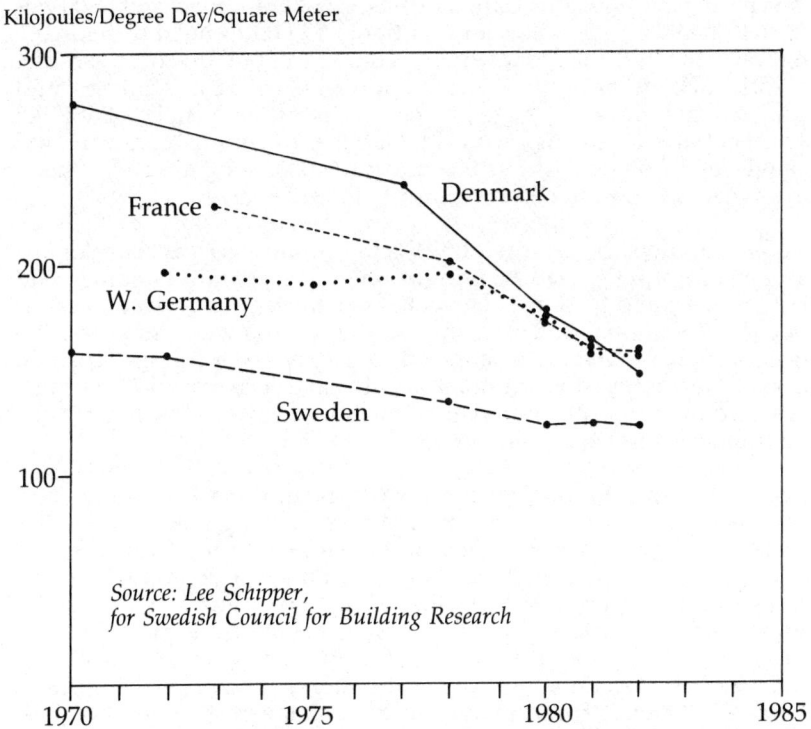

Figure 1: Efficiency Improvements in Residential Space Heating, 1970-82

on average, have twice the insulation values of homes in the northern state of Minnesota.[57]

The potential for improving the heat-saving capability of homes even in cold climates can be readily illustrated. C.A. Ficner of the Canadian Department of Energy, Mines, and Resources has compared costs in Canada of energy options in new homes of conventional design, energy-saving design, active solar heating, and passive solar heating.

A typical new house in Canada costs $80,000 to build and $800 per year to heat. By spending an additional $3,000 to build a thermally tighter structure, the cost of energy could be cut to $100 per year. The additional construction cost would add $450 per year in interest and principal to typical mortgage payments, giving an overall cost of $550. Thus net annual savings would total $250. In contrast, passive- and active-solar homes cost $92,000 and $100,000 to build. Their "heating" costs would total $2,200 and $3,300 per year.[58]

Conservation is the clear winner. Its importance is clear also: Almost 40 percent of all Canadian end-use energy goes into buildings and half of this could be saved. The benefits of energy conservation go far beyond the annual dollar savings to the houseowner, however. Reduced energy demand means reduced energy facility construction costs. The energy-efficient home would save society $7,000 in capital costs compared with a conventional house, even allowing for the additional cost to the homeowner.[59]

Similar benefits abound in the home appliance market. Energy cost increases for homeowners, coupled with some government policy measures, have increased efficiency since 1972 in the United States. Appliances for space heating, water heating, air conditioning, and refrigeration require three fourths of the energy used in U.S. buildings, with 42 percent going for space heat alone. Typical new gas furnaces now are about 70 percent efficient, having improved slightly over the last decade. New gas-fired systems, however, are up to 94 percent efficient. These employ heat exchangers that remove heat from flue gases by condensing them. Unfortunately, consumers usually choose the less efficient units.[60] (See Table 6.)

The seasonal efficiency of central air conditioners has improved by over 25 percent in the United States since 1972. Room air conditioners have also improved, by about 17 percent. The improvements occurred most dramatically between 1981 and 1982.[61]

Water heaters use 14 percent of the energy consumed in the U.S. buildings sector. But the efficiency of electric water heaters, which

Table 6: Efficiency of Typical U.S. Household Appliances Versus Best 1983/84 Models

	(percent)
Electric Heat Pump	53
Gas Furnace	50
Gas Water Heater	73
Electric Water Heater	35
Central Air Conditioner	84
Room Air Conditioner	64
Refrigerator	55
Freezer	73

Source: Howard S. Geller, "Efficient Residential Appliances and Space Conditioning Equipment: Current Savings Potential, Cost Effectiveness, and Research Needs," American Council for an Energy-Efficient Economy, Washington, D.C., July 1984.

represent a third of the market, declined between 1972 and 1980—by about 2 percent. (No data have been collected since that time, unfortunately, as a result of Reagan administration policy.) Typical natural gas-fired water heaters are only 48 percent efficient at point of use, compared with 80 percent for new pulse-combustion models. A new pulse-unit water heater would save over $115 per year in fuel in the average U.S. home.[62]

Refrigerators in Japan, even adjusted for smaller size, are twice as efficient as U.S. refrigerators. The Japanese refrigerators do not sacrifice frost-free features or other conveniences to attain efficiency. Rather, they have more efficient compressors, better design, and better insulation. The apparently higher efficiency of the Japanese refrigerator suggests that Japanese appliance makers could capture a sizable share of the U.S. market, just as the Japanese automakers did.[63]

More efficient appliances cost more to purchase, but they quickly pay for themselves. A highly efficient furnace may cost an additional $1,000, but it can yield an annual return on investment of 15 percent over an average model due to an efficiency improvement of 50 percent or more. A gas-fired water heater with an improvement of 33 percent over the average model in the United States costs up to $110 more, but it yields a rate of return of 35 percent per year. A refrigerator/freezer now on the market with an improvement of 20 percent yields an annual return of 52 percent. It costs only $60 more than models with average efficiencies.[64]

An Oak Ridge National Laboratory study in the southern United States showed that, even if an existing central air conditioning unit is not worn-out, replacing it can pay for the extra cost in only five years. Significantly, it was shown that many air conditioning units are over-sized, which leads to much energy waste from cycling losses. Over-sized units cost more to buy as well as to operate. Replacing the average worn-out unit with a properly sized efficient one pays for itself in 6-12 months in the southern United States and in 18-36 months in the mid-Atlantic states.[65]

Lighting in the United States costs about $30 billion in electricity each year, and consumes 25 percent of all electric power output. New ballasts to stabilize the current in the circuits of fluorescent lights can reduce energy costs by 20-25 percent, and replacing incandescent bulbs with small fluorescents can cut consumption by an estimated 75 percent. A recent article in the Electric Power Research Institute's *EPRI Journal* suggests that half the electricity used for lighting could be saved in the United States—420 billion kilowatt-hours per year. If accomplished, the savings would represent 0.5 percent of all world commercial energy, and 35 percent more electricity than the entire annual hydroelectric or nuclear power output of the United States. As the *EPRI Journal* put it, "[This energy] could be saved through energy-efficient strategies, all without imposing any hardships on productivity, safety, or esthetics."[66] For households, efficient new bulbs are available at a cost several times higher than incandescents, but they pay for themselves with energy savings and longer life. In many cases, new fluorescent fixtures must also be installed and these add a substantial cost. The life-cycle costs, however, remain favorable.

35

Commercial buildings use about one eighth of the energy consumed in the United States. Because lighting represents 40 percent of the peak electrical requirements for these buildings, peak loads on utilities could be cut sharply with lighting energy conservation. Lights also contribute much of the heat that must be removed by air conditioning. In fact, air conditioning is often required in these buildings in cold weather to remove the heat generated by excessive lighting. Audits and small investments in improvements in commercial buildings could yield electricity savings of 30 percent in lighting, 25 in space heat, 20 in air conditioning, and 15 percent for water heating.[67]

Swedish houses use 30-50 percent less heat than American homes. The Swedes enacted performance standards for residences in the mid-seventies and have offered incentives for conservation investments. Efficiency levels often exceed the requirements, though the standards may have increased awareness and accelerated the overall improvement. Analysts attribute the improvement to loans totaling more than $850 million made available for efficiency investments; to cooperation between homeowners, builders, and the government; to a national commitment to quality housing; to price increases; and to the new standards. They also noted that improvements were greater in homes built by those who inhabited them, as opposed to those who built homes to sell.[68]

The scope for saving energy in this sector is broad even where energy use in buildings is comparatively low, as is the case in the Soviet Union. The low usage is due in part to smaller living spaces, but also to the efficiency that is afforded by central heating systems. Many people live in cities in multifamily dwellings, permitting very efficient district heating. It also makes cogeneration possible, and the Soviets take good advantage of this opportunity. The United Nations has estimated, however, that an additional 20 percent savings could be attained in Soviet buildings by the year 2000. The study underscores the importance of conservation by noting that an increase of about 42 percent in total energy use by this sector is likely even if these savings are achieved, based on an assumption of rising living standards.[69]

The U.N. study also concluded that conservation could hold buildings sector energy demand in Western Europe to a rise of only 5 percent. Other research suggests a reduction in absolute energy use is possible. A Lawrence Berkeley Laboratory study estimates that with no change in energy prices, demand for energy per household in North America and Western Europe should remain constant. That is, increased demand for services as incomes grow would be offset by efficiency improvements. The author points out, too, that demand for most major energy services, or appliances, in these areas is saturated, and that the faster incomes grow, the sooner people can and will replace existing models with energy-efficient ones.[70] With rising prices and rising incomes, efficiency would improve faster.

In relative terms, Denmark, France, and West Germany have been most successful in improving efficiency in buildings, apparently because of a concerted and balanced commitment at the highest national levels to bring about energy savings. In the absence of balance, subsidies for conservation in the buildings sector in the form of direct grants have not been good policy. Billions of dollars worth of grants in Canada and the United Kingdom, for example, were not supplemented with information programs and were thus less effective than they might have been.[71] More fundamentally, a policy that assures rational energy pricing, backed with efficiency regulations in cases of classic market failure, offers the best hope of energy conservation in buildings.

Improving energy efficiency in residences in developing countries presents a very different sort of problem. The potential for conservation, however, is no less important. Fuelwood and charcoal provide two thirds of all energy used in Africa and a third of that used in Asia. Wood, in fact, supplies the equivalent of 15 million barrels of

"New stoves can cut wood
consumption by one fourth to one half."

37

oil per day, 80 percent of which is used for cooking. Indeed, one of the worst problems facing the developing world is the shrinking availability of fuel for cooking. As fuelwood becomes less available, the burden of collecting and transporting it, which usually falls on women and children, greatly adds to an already heavy work load. The economic burden is high where firewood is purchased rather than gathered. Firewood prices have risen over the last decade in India more than 2.5 percent per year above inflation. The widening circle of firewood collection, moreover, adds to the deforestation and soil erosion caused principally by lumbering, agriculture, and drought.[72]

The challenge is to improve the efficiency of cookstoves without adding to the work load, straining limited household budgets, diminishing sociocultural values, or reducing the utility of the cooking fire.[73] The fire is often simply an arrangement of three stones that support a cooking pot. Long, uncut branches or dung cakes are fed in from the unsheltered sides. The fire often serves as the center of family activity, though it rarely is needed for heat. Frequently, however, it is the only source of light.

Because the first step to more efficient wood use is to shelter the fire from the wind, the social and lighting functions of the fire can be compromised. Moreover, if the fire is enclosed in a stove, extra work is required to cut the wood to fit. The attraction of energy conservation, then, is partly offset by the loss of some amenities and the need for more work. But if a new stove cuts fuel consumption by one fourth to one half, as some suggest, then the time and effort of collecting fuel is greatly reduced. If the stove has a chimney, moreover, cooks are exposed to far less smoke and living spaces are made more comfortable.

One serious problem with stoves is that locally made versions often deteriorate to the point where they no longer save fuel. This is common where clay is used for construction. Reinforcing the clay or using scrap metal or ceramics to build the stove can improve performance. Another serious problem is that poor design leads to a mismatch between pots and the cooking holes into which they fit. Related difficulties are the failure to include enough cooking holes or the uneven distribution of heat among them, so that the cook is forced to spend more time preparing meals. Better design can solve these problems. Projects in El Salvador, Kenya, Nepal, and elsewhere have provided experience that will permit better design and production.[74]

The key to saving firewood and dung is low-cost, prefabricated stoves that are both durable and simple to use and service. The solution of technical problems alone, unfortunately, will not be sufficient, for the women who would most benefit from improved stoves usually cannot buy them. Until women share more control of family purse strings, this problem is not likely to disappear.

The use and conservation of kerosene and firewood in the home complicates energy policy in other sectors of developing country economies. Kerosene is often needed to supply light when stoves are substituted for open fires. Professor A. Reddy of the Indian Institute of Science points out that kerosene prices are regulated at low levels in India in order to provide lighting for many poor families. But kerosene is very similar to diesel fuel and will substitute for it in trucks. The price of diesel fuel, for this reason, must be set close to the price of kerosene. Thus, because fuel is cheap, more use is made of trucks for hauling freight than would be the case if diesel fuel were priced at market levels. Railroads could haul as much as 75 percent of Indian truck freight more efficiently. Reddy argues that the solution to this problem is rural household electrification to provide a substitute for kerosene for lighting, a change which would also be desirable because kerosene lighting is very inefficient. This approach was in fact undertaken successfully in South Korea. Though expensive and slow, this strategy may be necessary in many countries as a parallel effort to disseminate efficient wood stoves.[75]

The potential for improving the efficiency of the energy now consumed, largely in the form of non-commercial wood, dung, or crop wastes, is large and will offset some of the increase in the use of commercial fuels. Growth in commercial energy use in the homes of

"Without efficiency improvements,
global energy demand
will double by the year 2025."

the poor should not greatly affect the global energy budget simply because that use of energy is still so low. This is fortunate because energy's importance to development is clear. As Indian energy analyst, D.R. Pense, has written, "For what is removal of poverty or improvement in living standards all about, if even after thirty years of planning, it does not mean even a lighted home, a smoke-free kitchen, and water at the tap for the majority of people?"[76]

Counting Conservation's Potential

Two sharply contrasting visions of the world energy future have come into focus. On one hand, energy demand models based on past trends indicate that global demand will more than double by the year 2025. On the other, analyses based on an understanding of energy conservation show how demand could be held to a much smaller increase, stretching nonrenewable energy supplies and facilitating the use of renewable resources. Both visions have claim to validity, and the one that comes to pass will depend on conscious policy choices.

David Rose of the Massachusetts Institute of Technology analyzed these alternatives by applying the widely respected energy demand model created by Jae Edmonds and John Reilly of the Institute for Energy Analysis. Rose obtained energy demand results that differed by 100 percent depending on the amount of conservation assumed. But his study did not report the crucial impact that conservation had on energy prices—or the crucial effect that prices had on demand. Worldwatch Institute therefore asked Edmonds and Reilly to run their model using conservation improvements consistent with the potential demonstrated in this paper.[77]

Two scenarios were created for Worldwatch and contrasted with a third done previously for the U.S. Department of Energy (DOE). (See Table 7.) Most of the basic assumptions for economic growth, consumer price response and some 30-odd other factors were the same in all three: The world's economy and population were assumed to

Table 7: World Energy Consumption, and Carbon Dioxide and Sulfur Emissions, with Alternative Projections for 2000 and 2025

Scenario	Assumed Annual Energy Efficiency Improvement	Annual Energy Use	Annual Carbon Dioxide Emissions[1]	Annual Sulfur Emissions
	(percent)	(exajoules)	(billion tons)	(million tons)
1984 (actual)	2.3	300	5.0	100
YEAR 2000				
U.S. DOE Medium	0.8	460	7.2	170
Worldwatch Available Technology	1.8	360	5.8	120
Worldwatch New Technology	1.8	360	5.8	120
YEAR 2025				
U.S. DOE Medium	0.8	675	10.3	265
Worldwatch Available Technology	1.2	500	7.9	170
Worldwatch New Technology	1.8	450	7.0	135

[1]Measured in terms of carbon.

Sources: Worldwatch Institute. Assumptions are described in Notes 78 and 79, and J. Edmonds et al., *An Analysis of Possible Future Retention of Fossil Fuel CO_2* (Washington, D.C.: U.S. Department of Energy, September 1984).

grow until the year 2000 at annual rates of 3.2 and 1.2 percent, respectively. The only significant difference among the scenarios was the amount of energy conservation realized.[78]

The Worldwatch "available technology" scenario incorporated efficiency improvements rapid enough to make all countries by the end of the century as efficient as the most efficient countries today. It also assumed that the world economy would by the year 2025 be using the most efficient and economical energy-using devices currently available. No allowance was made for breakthroughs in energy efficiency. The annual improvement rates required to achieve these goals are 2 percent in industry and transportation and 1.5 percent for buildings until the year 2000, and then 1.2 percent for all sectors thereafter. In the Worldwatch "new technology" scenario, the higher rates of improvement are assumed to continue through new developments until the year 2025. The reference case, from the Department of Energy, assumes that efficiency will improve at only a 0.8 percent rate.[79]

The conservation contribution in the two models prepared for Worldwatch was impressive: the available technology scenario reduces energy growth by 175 exajoules annually in the year 2025, an amount equal to 60 percent of current world commercial energy use. The environmental importance of such an improvement can be seen in the quantity of sulfur produced under the different assumptions.

Acid-rain-forming sulfur emissions would, without controls, increase by 165 percent under the high energy scenario. Conservation could hold these releases to a 35 percent increase. Emissions control technologies still would be required, but their cost would be drastically reduced. It is likely that sulfur emissions are not the sole culprit in acid rain, but the link is strong enough to raise serious concern about rising emissions. Acid rain now threatens forests, aquatic life, and building materials throughout eastern North America and Europe. Without conservation and sulfur emissions controls, this threat could double.

The conservation scenarios would also reduce carbon dioxide emissions. Scientists agree that global climate changes will occur if atmospheric concentrations reach 600 parts per million (ppm). The pre-industrial level was only 280 ppm and the current level is 340 ppm. The U.S. DOE scenario would increase the concentration to 440 ppm and Worldwatch conservation scenarios would hold it to 410-420. Even decreasing the present level of carbon emissions significantly by using biomass energy on a massive scale would hold the carbon dioxide concentration only to 400 parts per million. The conservation scenarios would, however, reduce the buildup sufficiently to provide time to find a way to significantly cut back fossil fuel use.

The difference between the high and the low energy futures would have important economic and environmental consequences. Oil production equal to the current output of Saudi Arabia and Venezuela would be saved. Coal amounting to 40 percent more than the entire world uses today would be saved. Altogether, $2 trillion worth of energy would be saved in the year 2025, almost $300 per person. The cost of the conservation measures throughout the period would total only half the alternative of creating new supplies.

To achieve these savings, the world average energy efficiency in steel-making, for example, will by the year 2000 have to be equal to that of the Japanese today, and equal to the best currently available technology by the year 2025. Similar targets must be met for aluminum, paper, cement, and chemicals manufacture. Automobiles would have to average 31 miles per gallon by the end of the century and 45 mpg by 2025. Efficiency gains would permit the same amount of energy to provide twice as much space heat, hot water, air conditioning and refrigeration worldwide by the year 2025.

Yet this level of energy consumption would permit developing countries to share the amenities of energy use. Under these assumptions, incomes could grow to over $1,200 per capita in China and Africa and over $3,800 in Latin America. The cost of energy as a percent of incomes would change only slightly compared to today, partly because these nations can build efficiency into their economies as they develop.

"Conservation measures will cost
only half the alternative
of creating new supplies."

Major policy initiatives by all governments will be required to achieve the described conservation potential. The crucial policies to be implemented include market pricing of energy, elimination of subsidies for energy use, implementation of regulations to overcome market failures, provision of consumer information, research and development, and visible encouragement of conservation by leaders at all levels.

43

Preparing For An Energy Efficient Future

The pressures encouraging energy conservation are changing rapidly and are forcing a reconsideration of conservation policy. Oil prices have softened and incentives for conservation are expiring in many countries. The political will to impose and enforce efficiency regulations has diminished. The fiscal deficits of many governments mean that direct financial incentives are less affordable and that new conservation policy initiatives will have to be fashioned from tools that at least do not cost treasuries much money. Fortunately, the policies that have produced the largest efficiency improvements—energy pricing, taxation, and regulation—are compatible with these circumstances.

Energy price increases have stimulated more conservation than any other factor—witness the doubling of efficiency improvement rates following the two price hikes of the seventies. A detailed analysis of why energy use changed in the United States after 1973 reinforces this conclusion. Eric Hirst led a study at Oak Ridge National Laboratory that estimated the country now uses almost 20 percent less energy than it would have if policies had not changed. Energy price increases caused two thirds of the conservation response in the United States. Hirst and his co-authors suggest that the remaining third may be due to a variety of government measures such as automobile fuel economy standards.[80] The overall conservation response could have been greater but the United States was slow to decontrol oil prices, still controls the price of half of all natural gas used, and prices electric power at average costs, typically well below the cost of new power.

A similar analysis of the Canadian response to the energy crisis of the seventies produced similar results. Energy demand in Canada in 1982 was a third lower than would have been expected based on trends in effect in 1974. Of this reduction, a third was due to slower than expected economic growth, but two thirds has been attributed to responses to higher energy prices. The response could have been even greater, but Canada has adjusted prices slowly, and as recently as November 1984 held oil prices about 10 percent below the world level.[81]

The most energy efficient countries do not regulate energy prices. West Germany and Sweden price energy at the marginal, or replacement, cost, including natural gas and electricity. France, Italy, and Japan also have strong energy pricing policies. Major energy consuming nations that have weak energy pricing policies, policies that subsidize consumption far more than the United States or Canada, include the Soviet Union, China, and India. A third of the developing countries in a recent World Bank survey based energy prices on replacement costs, a third have mixed policies in which gasoline, for example, might be so priced but not electricity, and a third subsidize most forms of energy consumption. The result can be significant as suggested by the fact that Brazil and Mexico have virtually identical income levels but the latter, which subsidizes energy use heavily, uses twice as much energy per person as the former.[82]

Most oil importing developing countries pass on oil price increases directly and quickly. In the electricity sector, however, only 7 of 33 countries in the Third World surveyed recently by the World Bank applied marginal cost pricing to electricity. Price increases hit the rich, not the poor, because it is the former in developing countries that use most commercial energy.[83]

Some countries have recently reduced energy subsidies. The United States has eliminated the most important consumer subsidy, oil price controls, but continues to control the price of large quantities of natural gas. The World Bank has used its leverage to encourage the elimination of price subsidies wherever it could (particularly those for

44

gasoline), even denying loans in some instances to Egypt, Mexico, and Venezuela, partially because these countries subsidized energy prices. Recently, Brazil, Indonesia, the Ivory Coast, South Korea, and Turkey have moved to eliminate or trim measures that encourage energy waste, partly in response to pressure from the International Monetary Fund.[84] Some countries still apply failed energy policies, however, particularly in an effort to attract new industries. Australia, for example, recently agreed to supply hydroelectric power to the Aluminum Company of America at a rate that varies with the price of aluminum, an obvious subsidy of energy consumption. One result of this policy will be reduced pressure on aluminum consumers, most prominently the United States, to recycle aluminum in order to cut the energy costs of production.[85]

The most efficient nations are those that not only have accepted the reality of market prices but also bill energy consumers for the external costs of energy. These governments impose taxes to charge energy users for the burden to society their consumption represents, including the burden of environmental damage and of using foreign exchange to import oil. The tax on gasoline exceeds the price, for example, in Argentina, Belgium, Colombia, Netherlands, South Korea, and the United Kingdom. The tax in South Korea, in fact, exceeds $2 per gallon. Elsewhere, as in Japan, the tax on gasoline approaches $1 per gallon. New Zealand imposes a 50 percent excise tax on all automobiles with engines over 2 liters (122 cubic inches). When the tax was introduced in 1974, only 66 percent of new cars were smaller than 2 liters, but now 93 percent are smaller.[86]

Jae Edmonds points out, however, that energy scarcity alone may not be enough to encourage a level of conservation consistent with a low energy future. The widespread belief that an oil glut will persist for years has already diminished conservation efforts and may continue to do so. Price increases, moreover, will have little effect in centrally planned nations insulated from price signals or in regulated markets such as that for electric power. And as the world depends more on electricity, the role of markets in determining energy prices will diminish.[87]

There is the further problem of market failure. The classic case is the appliance bought by a landlord who does not pay the energy bill for operating it. The landlord has every incentive to buy the least costly furnace or water heater, not to pay more for one that will save energy costs. The tenant who will pay the energy bill has no say in the choice of appliance. Another example is the case of the more efficient but slightly more expensive automobile. Manufacturers could improve the fuel economy of their cars by 10-30 miles per gallon at an additional cost of $100-300 per vehicle, costs that would readily be repaid to the operator. They balk at doing so, however, fearing that the slightly higher purchase price will decrease sales. Consumers typically pay more attention to the purchase price of items than to potential life-cycle energy costs.

Regulatory policies can provide a minimum level of efficiency where markets fail or do not exist. The obvious targets for minimum performance standards are automobiles, furnaces, water heaters, air conditioners, and heat pumps. Automakers, for example, could reasonably be required to increase fuel economy to 30 and 45 miles per gallon by, respectively, 1990 and the end of the century.

Such standards could be very useful in developing as well as developed countries. They would help ease the burden that energy imports—and borrowed capital for new energy supply systems—impose upon foreign exchange. Many enery-using devices, especially cars, air conditioners, and refrigerators, could be regulated both in domestic manufacturing plants and as imports to ensure that the most efficient ones are purchased.

Fuel economy standards could play a vital role in the developed world. Sweden has set a goal of 31 mpg by 1990 for auto fuel economy, and has conducted negotiations with 11 auto manufacturers and importers in order to assure this goal is met. Japan has had a voluntary standard of 31 mpg, but the mandatory U.S. standards will not increase beyond 27.5 mpg, and may even be rolled back from this level. No single measure would be more productive than a 45 mpg standard for all major gasoline consuming nations. Minimum per-

"Obvious targets for minimum
efficiency standards are automobiles,
furnaces, water heaters, and air conditioners."

formance levels might also be required for industries in centrally planned economies, although the complexity of such standards as well as redundancy makes them undesirable in market economies. The standards chosen for all items should be based on marginal energy costs, including the environmental and other external costs of energy. As Clark Bullard of the University of Illinois suggests, regulatory policy seldom can take society beyond the economically desirable levels, and indeed should not do so. Nevertheless, regulations can provide an insurance policy against failure.[88]

47

New technological developments will be necessary to attain the more efficient Worldwatch scenario. Promising areas for research lie in the development of new materials for making lighter automobiles, high-temperature sensing and control systems, large heat pumps, and entirely new industrial processes. Industry support for research varies widely by category, with the iron and steel and the paper industries spending relatively very little. U.S. Government support for energy conservation research has declined precipitously because of Reagan administration cuts. But as the Worldwatch available technology scenario suggests, the greatest opportunity for conservation lies in putting known measures into practice. Innovations of this type will depend heavily on the spread of information on their value and availability.[89]

Many countries in both the East and West have implemented a variety of energy conservation incentives, information, and assistance programs. Efficiency labeling of energy consuming products such as automobiles, furnaces, and refrigerators has been a very useful government function in Sweden, the United States, and Western Europe. Other measures such as voluntary efficiency goals, efficiency audits, and grant programs have a mixed record of achievement, having worked well in Sweden, Canada, and Denmark, and less well elsewhere. The success of these programs seems to depend on national leadership, for they are taken most seriously when popular leaders elevate their importance. Where incentives are expiring, as in the United States and West Germany, policymakers should keep a close watch on the performance of their economies in energy efficiency and be prepared to reinstitute measures if efforts weaken.

Policymakers are thus presented with the task of making energy policy on numerous fronts. Many industries, services, and, finally, people will be affected in complex, sometimes conflicting ways. But the most important policies reduce to a few manageable items, and the most important benefits clearly are worth the effort.

Leaders can think of conservation in many ways. They can view it as a way to maintain their nation's competitive position in the world economy, and as a way to improve trade balances by either reducing the need to import energy or freeing up extra fuel for export. Conservation can be considered a way to promote economic growth by cutting capital requirements for energy and thus making funds available for more productive economic investments elsewhere. And they can view conservation as a preventive for forest damage as a result of acid rain, and all the other environmental problems caused by energy use.

In countries with large deficits, energy taxes may offer an important option. These taxes would help stabilize declining energy prices and maintain the impetus to conserve. Very poor citizens would need shelter from these taxes and increased prices, however, through life-line utility rates—low-price electricity to meet basic needs—and income transfers.[90]

Critics of pricing policies argue that they can only hurt the poor, and that taxation would make matters worse. It is true that the United States has failed to provide sufficient income transfers or conservation assistance to make up to the poor their loss due to energy price increases, and they as a result are worse off than before. The long run value even to the poor of market pricing of energy can be seen, however, in the scenarios described above. The price of oil is several dollars per barrel lower in the conservation scenarios than in the U.S. DOE scenario. The application of energy taxes in the early years of the period and their maintenance would set and hold the world on a course of conservation. Unless prices are stabilized, the current situation could start a new cycle of energy consumption growth and rapid price increases. No segment of society would benefit more from long-term stability in oil prices than the developing countries, where two thirds the world's population resides.[91]

The risk of failure in conserving energy, whether from undue pessimism or failure of will, is great. The risk includes overbuilding energy facilities, overstressing energy capital budgets, and overburdening the environment. It is a risk that need not be borne.

Notes

1. For a discussion of energy demand modeling, see Part I of John H. Gibbons and William U. Chandler, *Energy: The Conservation Revolution* (New York: Plenum Press, 1981) and Charles J. Hitch, ed., *Modeling Energy-Economy Interactions* (Washington, D.C.: Resources for the Future, 1977).

2. See U.S. National Academy of Sciences, *Changing Climate: Report of the Carbon Dioxide Assessment Committee* (Washington, D.C.: National Academy Press, 1983), Stephen Seidel and Dale Keyes, *Can We Delay A Greenhouse Warming?* (Washington, D.C.: U.S. Environmental Protection Agency, September 1983), and William W. Kellogg and Robert Schware, "Society, Science and Climate Change," *Foreign Affairs*, Summer 1982.

3. An international survey of 328 organizations that have published energy demand projections was undertaken for the International Energy Workshop. The "median" projection for the year 2000 was 485 exajoules. See Alan S. Manne and Leo Schrattenholzer, "International Energy Workshop: A Summary of the 1983 Poll Responses," *The Energy Journal*, Vol. 5, No. 1, 1984. For projections beyond the year 2000 commonly used in analysis of the global carbon dioxide problem, see J. Edmonds et al., *An Analysis of Possible Future Atmospheric Retention of Fossil Fuel CO_2* (Washington, D.C.: U.S. Department of Energy, September 1984).

4. Both the Manne quote and the survey information are found in Manne and Schrattenholzer, "International Energy Workshop: 1983 Poll Responses." The survey results can be compared with world energy demand projections published by the Workshop on Alternative Energy Strategies, *Energy Supply-Demand Integrations to the Year 2000* (Cambridge, Mass.: MIT Press, 1977) and World Energy Conference (WEC), Conservation Commission, *Report on World Energy Demand, 1985-2020* (London: World Energy Conference, 1977). Individual scenarios from these pre-Iranian crisis studies that assumed 3-4 percent annual economic growth and, in the WEC study, "high" energy price elasticity, yielded results only 14 percent higher than the Manne survey's estimate of the median projection today.

5. See Scenario B, Appendix, in Edmonds et al., *Possible Future Atmospheric Retention of CO_2*.

6. For a discussion of the CO_2 problems, see reference 2. Regarding hydropower's impacts, see for example, William U. Chandler, *The Myth of TVA: Conservation and Development in the Tennessee Valley, 1933-1983* (Cambridge, Mass.: Ballinger Publishing Company, 1984); Edward Goldsmith and Nich-

olas Hildyard, *The Social and Environmental Effects of Large Dams, Volume 1* (Cornwall, U.K.: The Wadebridge Ecological Centre, 1984); Martin Weil, "Hydropower," *The China Business Review*, July/August, 1982; Paul Aspelin and Silvio Coelho dos Santos, *Indian Areas Threatened by Hydroelectric Projects in Brazil* (Copenhagen, Denmark: International Work Group for Indigenous Affairs, 1981).

7. M. Desmond Fitzgerald and Gerald Pollio, "Financing Energy Developments 1983-2000," Chemical Bank, New York, undated.

8. Commercial energy use by 15 countries from World Bank, *World Development Report 1984* (New York: Oxford University Press, 1984); United Nations Economic Commission for Europe (UNECE), *An Energy Efficient Future: Prospects for Europe and North America* (London: Butterworths, 1983); U.S. savings with most-efficient lights from Nadine Lihach and Stephen Pertusiello, "Evolution in Lighting," *EPRI Journal*, June 1984; Energy Information Administration (EIA), *International Energy Annual 1982* (Washington, D.C.: Department of Energy, 1983).

9. UNECE, *An Energy Efficient Future*; Andrea N. Ketoff (International Energy Studies, Lawrence Berkeley Laboratory, Berkeley, Calif.), "Facts and Prospects of the Italian End-Use Energy Structure," Rolf Bauerschmidt (Institute for Applied Systems Analysis and Prognosis, Hanover, West Germany), "An End-Use Oriented Energy Strategy for the Federal Republic of Germany," and Jean Marie Martin (Institute Economique et Juridique de l'Energie), "Alternative Energy Strategies for France," presented at the Global Workshop on End-Use Energy Strategies, São Paulo, Brazil, June 4-15, 1984.

10. Marc Ross, "Industrial Energy Conservation," *Natural Resources Journal*, April 1984.

11. Haruki Tsuchiya (Research Institute for Systems Technology, Tokyo, Japan), "Case Study on Japan," presented at the Global Workshop on End-Use Energy Strategies, São Paulo, Brazil, June 4-15, 1984; World Bank, *Energy Efficiency in the Steel Industry with Emphasis on the Developing Countries* (Washington, D.C.: 1984).

12. Martin, "Alternative Energy Strategies for France."

13. Energy intensity of U.S. production from Ross, "Industrial Energy Conservation"; Ketoff, "Italian End-Use Energy Structure"; Bauerschmidt, "End-Use Strategy for Federal Republic of Germany."

14. José Goldemberg et al., "Brazil: A Study on End-Use Energy Strategy," presented at the Global Workshop on End-Use Energy Strategies, São Paulo, Brazil, June 4-15 1984; UNECE, *An Energy Efficient Future*; World Bank, *Energy Efficiency in the Steel Industry*.

15. Ketoff, "Italian End-Use Energy Structure"; Spain's efficiency in steelmaking from World Bank, *Energy Efficiency in the Steel Industry*; use of electric arc furnace from Jack R. Miller, "Steel Minimills," *Scientific American*, May 1984; steel recycling from imports, and world rate, from William U. Chandler, *Materials Recycling: The Virtue of Necessity* (Washington, D.C.: Worldwatch Institute, October 1983).

16. Various rates of return on investments from World Bank, *Energy Efficiency in the Steel Industry* and from U.S. Office of Technology Assessment (OTA), *Industrial Energy Use* (Washington, D.C.: U.S. Government Printing Office, June 1983); Ross, "Industrial Energy Conservation."

17. U.S. use of open hearth furnace from OTA, *Industrial Energy Use*; other countries from World Bank, *Energy Efficiency in the Steel Industry*.

18. World Bank, *Energy Efficiency in the Steel Industry*.

19. UNECE, *An Energy Efficient Future*.

20. Ed A. Hewett, *Energy, Economics, and Foreign Policy in the Soviet Union* (Washington, D.C.: Brookings Institution, 1984); Sumer C. Aggarwal, "Managing Material Shortages: The Russian Way," *Columbia Journal of World Business*, Fall 1980.

21. The uncertainty regarding the rate of introduction of recycling technology is indicated in news stories such as "The Steelworkers Dig in Against a Cleveland Minimill," *Business Week*, January 23, 1984, and Steven Greenhouse, "Minimills: Steel's Bright Star," *New York Times*, February 24, 1984.

22. The implied rate of efficiency improvement in the mid-range projection of Edmonds et al., *Possible Future Atmospheric Retention of CO_2* (Scenario B) is 0.8 percent per year. If efficiency improvements in Soviet steel-making were consistent with this rate, it would require 68 years to reduce the current level of energy use per ton in the Soviet Union (31 gigajoules) to the current Japanese level (18 gigajoules). Brazilian plans from Goldemberg et al., "Brazil: End-Use Strategy."

54

23. Miller, "Steel Minimills"; Donald F. Barnett and Louis Schorsch, *Steel: Upheaval in a Basic Industry* (Cambridge, Mass.: Ballinger Publishing Co., 1983); F.T. Sparrow, *Energy and Materials Flows in the Iron and Steel Industry* (Springfield, Va.: National Technical Information Service, April 1982); OTA, *Industrial Energy Use* ; World Bank, *Energy Efficiency in the Steel Industry.*

24. OTA, *Industrial Energy Use*; World Bank, *Energy Efficiency in the Steel Industry.* Note that capital costs are given in terms of tons of annual production capacity, and that total cost includes energy, labor, and amortized capital on a per-ton-produced basis.

25. Goldemberg et al., "Brazil: End-Use Strategy."

26. Chandler, *Materials Recycling: The Virtue of Necessity.*

27. Tsuchiya, "Case Study on Japan."

28. S.Y. Shen, *Energy and Materials Flows in the Production of Primary Aluminum* (Springfield, Va.: National Technical Information Service, October 1981); United Nations Environment Programme, "Industry and Environment," Nairobi, Kenya, August/September 1983; Organisation for Economic Co-operation and Development (OECD), *Aluminum Industry: Energy Aspects of Structural Change* (Paris: 1983); Goldemberg et al., "Brazil: End-Use Strategy"; UNECE, *An Energy Efficient Future*; Bauerschmidt, "End-Use Strategy for Federal Republic of Germany."

29. For an overview of industrial energy conservation, see Melvin H. Chiogioji, *Industrial Energy Conservation* (New York: Marcel Dekker, Inc., 1979).

30. Howard S. Geller, "The Potential for Electricity Conservation in Brazil," American Council for an Energy-Efficient Economy, Washington, D.C., February 1984, draft.

31. N. Mohan, "Techniques for Energy Conservation in AC Motor-Drive Systems," prepared for the Electric Power Research Institute, Palo Alto, California, September 1981.

32. OTA, *Industrial Energy Use.*

33. Quote is from H.N. Hersh, *Energy and Materials Flows in the Production of Pulp and Paper* (Springfield, Va.: National Technical Information Service, May 1981).

34. Chandler, *Materials Recycling: The Virtue of Necessity.*

35. Bauerschmidt, "End-Use Strategy for Federal Republic of Germany." The energy intensity of German industry declined at an annual rate of 4.6 percent per year after 1979. Rates of return on chemical industry investments from OTA, *Industrial Energy Use.*

36. "PET Plastic Recovery," *Resource Recycling*, March/April 1983; L.L. Gaines and S.Y. Shen, *Energy and Materials Flows in the Production of Olefins and Their Derivatives* (Springfield, Va.: National Technical Information Service, August 1980).

37. J.E. Sapp, *Energy and Materials Flows in the Cement Industry* (Springfield, Va.: National Technical Information Service, June 1981); U.S. cement production and energy consumption from U.S. Department of Interior, Bureau of Mines, *Minerals Yearbook, 1982, Volume 1* (Washington, D.C.: U.S. Government Printing Office, 1983); Hewett, *Energy, Economics, and Foreign Policy in the Soviet Union*; Hugh Saddler, "Energy Supply and Demand in Australia: A Statistical Compendium," presented at the Global Workshop on End-Use Energy Strategies, São Paulo, Brazil, June 4-15, 1984; West European data from Bureau of Mines, *Minerals Yearbook, Vol. 1, 1982.*

38. Derived from Edmonds et al., *Possible Future Atmospheric Retention of CO_2* and from UNECE, *An Energy Efficient Future.*

39. These estimates assume that the average world car is driven 8,500 miles per year, obtains 21 miles per gallon of fuel, and that approximately 353 million cars exist. The assumptions for U.S. cars are 10,000 miles per year, 16 miles per gallon, and 125 million cars.

40. UNECE, *An Energy Efficient Future.*

41. James Bruce, "Brazilian Automakers Prepare for New Boom," *Journal of Commerce*, July 31, 1984; Goldemberg et al., "Brazil: End-Use Strategy."

42. Cost of conservation estimated by Worldwatch Institute, but see also OTA, *Increased Automobile Fuel Efficiency and Synthetic Fuels* (Washington, D.C.: U.S. Government Printing Office, 1982); Charles Gray, Jr. and Frank von Hippel, "The Fuel Economy of Light Vehicles," *Scientific American*, May 1981.

43. R. Feast, "Volvo Shows its Car of the Future," *Automotive News,* July 4, 1983; D. Scott and J. Yamaguchi, "High Performance with Economy Engine in Ultra-Light Body," *Automotive Engineering,* April 1983; J.P. Norbye, "Light-Weight Fuel-Sipper Gets 56 mpg," *Popular Science,* March 1982, as cited in Goldemberg et al., "Brazil: End-Use Strategy." For a critical comment on the proposed rule changes in U.S. fuel economy standards, see Norris Mc-Donald, "Petition for Reconsideration: Light Truck Average Fuel Economy Standards 49 CRF Part 533 Docket FE 78-01," Environmental Policy Institute, November 21, 1984; and Warren Brown, "GM, Ford Seek Relief In Mileage," *Washington Post,* July 31, 1984.

44. Goldemberg et al., "Brazil: End-Use Strategy."

45. Jose Lutzenberger, Union for the Conservation of Nature, Rio Grande do Sul, Brazil, private communication, September 20, 1984; Roger Cans, "Canne á Sucre Contre Piranhas," *Le Monde,* December 2/3, 1984.

46. These calculations assume the average fuel economy of cars in Brazil is about 20 miles per gallon, that cars are driven about 9,300 miles per year, and that car ownership grows at 5 percent. This growth assumption represents a considerable decline from the 7 percent of the last five years, which was notable for continued high growth in auto ownership despite the severe recession. The actual growth rate has declined, however, from about 12 percent per year during the seventies. See note 41.

47. See, "GM Says It Will Launch CVT In Europe Soon," *Ward's Engine Update,* July 1, 1983, as cited in Goldemberg et al., "Brazil: End-Use Strategy." But note also that problems with the mass production of CVTs has caused $30 million overruns at Van Doane Transmissie in Holland. The company is being reorganized to increase efficiency; see *Ward's Automotive Reports,* August 27, 1984, as cited in the U.S. Department of Energy, *Monthly Data Report,* September 14, 1984. William U. Chandler, "The Fuel Efficiency of Tires by Manufacturer and Model," Environmental Policy Institute, Washington, D.C., September 1981.

48. Bauerschmidt, "End-Use Strategy for Federal Republic of Germany."

49. UNECE, *An Energy Efficient Future.*

50. Ibid.

51. R.I. Salawu (University of Lagos, Nigeria), "End Use Energy Study, Nigeria," presented at the Global Workshop on End-Use Energy Strategies, São Paulo, Brazil, June 4-15, 1984.

52. See, for example, Gabriel Roth and George G. Wynne, *Learning from Abroad: Free Enterprise Urban Transportation* (London: Transaction Books, 1982), Herbert H. Werlin, "Urban Transportation Systems in the Developing World," *Ekistics*, May/June 1984, and J. Diandas, "Alternative Approaches to Transport in Third World Cities: Issues in Equity and Accessibility," *Ekistics*, May/June 1984.

53. V.M. Maslenikov, "Specific Features of the Development of the USSR Fuel-and-Energy Complex" presented at the Global Workshop on End-Use Energy Strategies, São Paulo, Brazil, June 4-15, 1984; UNECE, *An Energy Efficient Future*; Hewett, *Energy, Economics, and Foreign Policy in the Soviet Union*.

54. Goldemberg et al., "Brazil: End-Use Strategy."

55. Problems with U.S. railroads from Al Lewis, former Vice President, Louisville and Nashville Railroad, private communication, 1976; construction of waterways to compete with rail from Chandler, *The Myth of TVA*.

56. From Lee Schipper, *Internationell Jaemfoerelse av Bostaedernads Energifoerbrukning* (Stockholm: Swedish Council for Building Research, 1984). An English version and summary was submitted to *Energy Economics*, Journal of the International Association of Energy Economists. According to Schipper, figures are calculated in terms of useful energy/degree day/square meter of floorspace. Floor space estimates include all dwellings and are somewhat uncertain. Useful energy is derived from actual energy consumed, figuring liquid and gaseous fuels at 66 percent conversion efficiency, electricity and district heating at 100 percent efficiency, wood and coal at 55 percent efficiency. The actual mix of fuels varies considerably from country to country and over time. See also, Bent Petersen, "The Danish Energy-Conservation Program in Buildings," in American Council for an Energy-Efficient Economy (ACEEE), *Doing Better: Setting an Agenda for the Second Decade, Vol. J* (Proceedings from the Panel on Programs Outside of the United States) (Washington, D.C.: 1984).

57. Lee Schipper, "Residential Energy Use in the OECD: 1970-1982—The Bottom-Up Approach," and Lee Schipper, "Energy Efficient Housing in Sweden," in ACEEE, *Doing Better, Vol. J*.

58. Charles A. Ficner, "The Evolution Towards R-2000: Past Experiences and Current Directions of the Canadian Energy Conservation Effort," in ACEEE, *Doing Better, Vol. J.*

59. Savings estimated by Worldwatch from Ficner, "The Evolution Towards R-2000," and from EIA, *International Energy Annual 1982.*

60. John P. Kesselring, Robert M. Kendall, and Richard J. Schreiber, "Radiant Fiber Burners for Gas-Fired Appliances and Equipment," and William H. Thrasher, Robert J. Kolodgy, and James J. Fuller, "Development of a Space Heater and a Residential Water Heater Based on the Pulse Combustion Principle," in ACEEE, *Doing Better, Vol. E* (Proceedings from the Panel on Appliances and Equipment).

61. Howard S. Geller, "Efficient Residential Appliances and Space Conditioning Equipment: Savings Potential and Cost Effectiveness as of 1984," in ACEEE, *Doing Better, Vol. E.*

62. Anthony Usibelli, "Monitored Energy Use of Residential Water Heaters," in ACEEE, *Doing Better, Vol. E*; Thrasher, Kolodgy, and Fuller, "The Pulse Combustion Principle."

63. David B. Goldstein, "Efficient Refrigerators in Japan: A Comparative Survey of American and Japanese Trends Towards Energy Conserving Refrigerators," in ACEEE, *Doing Better, Vol. E.*

64. Geller, "Efficient Residential Appliances and Space Conditioning Equipment."

65. Howard A. McLain and David Goldemberg, "Benefits of Replacing Residential Central Air Conditioning Systems," in ACEEE, *Doing Better, Vol. E.*

66. Rudy R. Verderber and Francis M. Rubinstein, "New Lighting Technologies, Their Status and Impacts on Power Densities," in ACEEE, *Doing Better, Vol. E*; hydroelectric output from EIA, *International Energy Annual 1982*; Lihach and Pertusiello, "Evolution in Lighting."

67. Betsy L. Gardiner, Mary Ann Piette, and Jeffrey P. Harris, "Measured Results of Energy Conservation Retrofits in Non-Residential Buildings: An Update of the BECA-CR Data Base," and Donald K.Schultz, "End Use Consumption Patterns and Energy Conservation Savings in Commercial Buildings," in ACEEE, *Doing Better, Vol. D* (Proceedings from the Panel on Existing Commercial Buildings).

68. Schipper, "Energy Efficient Housing in Sweden"; Lars Engebeck, "Are Building Codes Effective Tools for Reducing Energy Use in New Residential Buildings? Some Swedish Experiences," in ACEEE, *Doing Better, Vol. J.*

69. David Wilson, *The Demand for Energy in the Soviet Union* (London: Croom Helm, 1983); Hewett, *Energy, Economics, and Foreign Policy in the Soviet Union*; UNECE, *An Energy Efficient Future.*

70. Schipper, "Residential Energy Use in the OECD."

71. See Dennis C. Anderson, "Evaluation of Canada's Oil Substitution Program," and Ian Brown, "The Administration of Energy Conservation Programmes by Western European Governments," in ACEEE, *Doing Better, Vol. J.*

72. Bina Agarwal, "Why Stoves are Resisted," *Unasylva*, No. 140, 1983. For a description of recent trends in soil erosion, see Lester R. Brown and Edward C. Wolf, *Soil Erosion: Quiet Crisis in the World Economy* (Washington, D.C.: Worldwatch Institute, September 1984); Economic Intelligence Service, *Current Energy Scene in India* (Centre for Monitoring Indian Economy: May 1983); and Erik Eckholm, Gerald Foley, Geoffrey Barnard, and Lloyd Timberlake, *Fuelwood: The Energy Crisis That Won't Go Away* (London: Earthscan, 1984).

73. For a severe critique of wood-stove efficiency projects, see Gerald Foley and Patricia Moss, *Improved Cooking Stoves in Developing Countries* (London: International Institute for Environment and Development, 1983).

74. See, for example, Gyan Sagar, "A Fuel-Efficient, Smokeless Stove for Rural India," *Appropriate Technology*, September 1980; "Stove Design" and "Stove Dissemination," *VITA News*, January 1984; George McBean, "Sushila Wants a New Stove," *UNICEF News*, Issue 3, 1983; John Worral, "Better Stoves Help Solve Firewood Crisis," *Christian Science Monitor*, March 14, 1984.

75. Amulya Kumar N. Reddy, "A Strategy for Resolving India's Oil Crisis," *Current Science*, January 20, 1981.

76. D.R. Pendse, "Dilemmas of Energy Strategies in India: Implications for Third World," *Economic and Political Weekly*, March 31, 1984.

77. David J. Rose, *Global Energy Futures and CO₂-Induced Climate Change, Chapters 1-8 and Appendices* (Cambridge, Mass.: MIT Department of Nuclear Engineering, November 1983). The model has also been used in Seidel and Keyes, *Can We Delay a Greenhouse Warming?*

78. All assumptions and results for the DOE "medium" scenario (referred to as "B" in the citation) are described in detail in Edmonds et al., *Atmospheric Retention of CO_2*. Full details of the Available Technology and New Technology scenarios are available from Worldwatch upon request. The following key assumptions were the same in all projections: Population grows at about 1 percent per year from 1984 to 2025. Gross World Product grows annually at 3.15 percent until 2000, then slows to 2.6 percent. Price elasticity of demand for energy services is -0.9 in the buildings sector, -0.8 in the industrial sector, and -0.7 in the transportation sector in the OECD countries, and is -0.8 for all sectors in the rest of the world (for all years). Income elasticity of demand for energy is 0.8 for all regions (for all years). Primary energy prices are determined endogenously, and thus differ by scenario. Oil prices through 2000 increase annually in DOE's Scenario B, Worldwatch Available Technology, and Worldwatch New Technology at 1.7, 1.2, and 0.9 percent, and from 2000 to 2025 at 1.7, 1.7, and 1.6 percent, respectively. Coal and biomass prices never increase above 0.8 percent annually in DOE's Scenario B or above 0.6 percent in either Worldwatch projection. The cost of nuclear-electric, hydro-electric, and solar-electric power changes at 1.6, 0, and -5.2 percent annually in all cases. Sulfur emissions are estimated by assuming an average sulfur content of coal of 2 percent.

79. The incorporation of efficiency improvements was accomplished in the model by adjusting the rate of non-price-induced conservation as well as energy prices. The latter required an artificial shift in the supply curve, or the equivalent of an energy tax. For comparison, the energy demand projection for the United States grew from about 75 exajoules in the year 1983 (note that in the model all values are based on 1975) to 105, 85, and 83 exajoules in the DOE, Available Technology, and New Technology Scenarios, respectively. This compares with a range of 81 to 92 exajoules in *The Audubon Energy Plan 1984* (New York: National Audubon Society, July 1984).

80. Eric Hirst et al., "Recent Changes in U.S. Energy Consumption: What Happened and Why," in Annual Reviews, Inc., *Annual Review of Energy* (Palo Alto, Calif.: 1983).

81. John F. Helliwell, Mary E. MacGregor, and Andre Plourde, "Changes in Canadian Energy Demand, Supply, and Policies, 1974-1986," *Natural Resources Journal,* April 1984; Fred Langan, "From Gasoline Tax Hike to Defense Cuts, Canada Tightens Its Belt," *Christian Science Monitor,* November 14, 1984.

82. International Energy Agency, *Energy Policies and Programmes of IEA Countries, 1983 Review* (Paris: Organisation for Economic Cooperation and Development, 1984); High-Level Expert Group Meetings Preparatory to the Fourth General Conference of UNIDO, Energy and Industrialization, Oslo, Norway, 29 August-2 September 1983, "The Economics of, and Potential For, Energy Conservation and Substitution," United Nations Industrial Development Organization, August 9, 1983; *World Bank Development Report, 1984.*

83. *The Energy Transition in Developing Countries* (Washington, D.C.: World Bank, August 1983).

84. Yves Albouy, World Bank, private communication, November 8, 1984.

85. Richard Anderson, "Aussies Gamble on Aluminum," *Energy Daily,* August 10, 1984, and "Aluminum Smelter Project Resuscitated in Australia," *Journal of Commerce,* August 1, 1984.

86. International Energy Agency, *Energy Policies and Programmes of IEA Countries, 1983 Review;* Lester R. Brown et al., *State of the World, 1984* (New York: W.W. Norton, Inc., 1984).

87. Jae Edmonds, Institute for Energy Analysis, private communication, Washington, D.C., October 24, 1984.

88. Clark W. Bullard, "Energy Conservation in New Buildings: Opportunities, Experience, and Options," *Annual Review of Energy* (Palo Alto, Calif.: Annual Reviews, Inc., 1981).

89. Energy Research Advisory Board, "Energy Conservation and the Federal Government: Research, Development, and Management," Report to the U.S. Department of Energy, Washington, D.C., January 1983.

90. Mohan Munasinghe, "Third World Energy Policies: Demand Management and Conservation," *Energy Policy*, March 1983.

91. Phil O'Keefe and Lars Kristoferson, "The Uncertain Energy Path—Energy and Third World Development," *Ambio*, Vol. 13, No. 3; George F. Ray, "European Energy Alternatives and Future Developments," *Natural Resources Journal*, April 1984.

WILLIAM U. CHANDLER is a Senior Researcher at Worldwatch Institute in Washington, D.C. He is co-author of *Energy: The Conservation Revolution* and author of *The Myth of TVA*, as well as many articles on energy and the environment.

THE WORLDWATCH PAPER SERIES

No. of
Copies

Single Copy—$4.00

Bulk Copies (any combination of titles)
2-5: $3.00 each   5-20: $2.00 each   21 or more: $1.00 each

Calendar Year Subscription (1984 subscription begins with Paper 58)
U.S. $25.00 _____

Make check payable to Worldwatch Institute
1776 Massachusetts Avenue NW, Washington, D.C. 20036 USA

Enclosed is my check for U.S. $ _____

_____

name
_____

address
_____

city   **state**   **zip/country**

four dollars

Worldwatch Institute
1776 Massachusetts Avenue, N.W.
Washington, D.C. 20036 USA